Franklin D. Roosevelt

by Rebecca Pettiford

BELLWETHER MEDIA • MINNEAPOLIS, MN

Blastoff! Readers are carefully developed by literacy experts to build reading stamina and move students toward fluency by combining standards-based content with developmentally appropriate text.

 Level 1 provides the most support through repetition of high-frequency words, light text, predictable sentence patterns, and strong visual support.

 Level 2 offers early readers a bit more challenge through varied sentences, increased text load, and text-supportive special features.

 Level 3 advances early-fluent readers toward fluency through increased text load, less reliance on photos, advancing concepts, longer sentences, and more complex special features.

★ **Blastoff! Universe**

Reading Level

Grade **K**

Grades **1–3**

Grade **4**

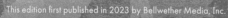

This edition first published in 2023 by Bellwether Media, Inc.

No part of this publication may be reproduced in whole or in part without written permission of the publisher. For information regarding permission, write to Bellwether Media, Inc., Attention: Permissions Department, 6012 Blue Circle Drive, Minnetonka, MN 55343.

Library of Congress Cataloging-in-Publication Data

Names: Pettiford, Rebecca, author.
Title: Franklin D. Roosevelt / by Rebecca Pettiford.
Description: Minneapolis, MN : Bellwether Media, Inc., 2023. | Series: Blastoff! readers: American presidents | Audience: Ages 5-8 | Audience: Grades 2-3 | Summary: "Relevant images match informative text in this introduction to Franklin D. Roosevelt. Intended for students in kindergarten through third grade"-- Provided by publisher.
Identifiers: LCCN 2022001062 (print) | LCCN 2022001063 (ebook) | ISBN 9781644877067 (library binding) | ISBN 9781648348723 (paperback) | ISBN 9781648347528 (ebook)
Subjects: LCSH: Roosevelt, Franklin D. (Franklin Delano), 1882-1945--Juvenile literature. | Presidents--United States--Biography--Juvenile literature.
Classification: LCC E807 .P48 2023 (print) | LCC E807 (ebook) | DDC 973.917092 [B]--dc23/eng/20220112
LC record available at https://lccn.loc.gov/2022001062
LC ebook record available at https://lccn.loc.gov/2022001063

Editor: Rachael Barnes   Series Designer: Jeffrey Kollock   Book Designer: Gabriel Hilger

Printed in the United States of America, North Mankato, MN.

Table of Contents

Who Was Franklin D. Roosevelt?

Franklin D. Roosevelt was the 32nd president of the United States.

4

He served from 1933 to 1945. His presidency was the longest in U.S. history!

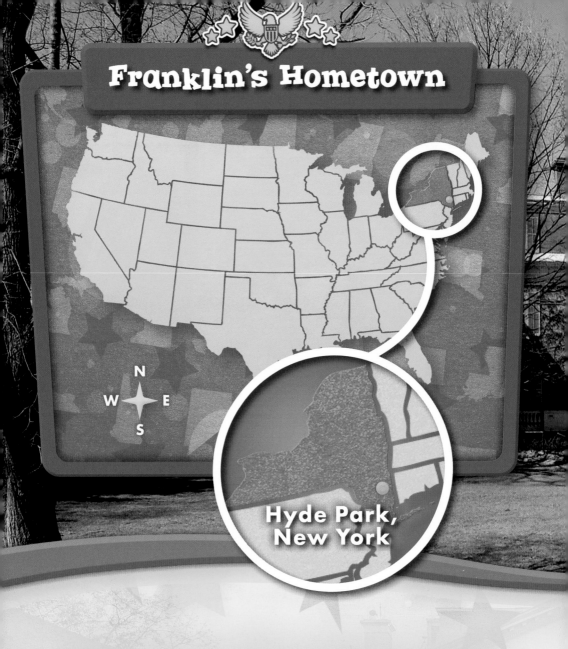

Franklin's Hometown

Hyde Park,
New York

Franklin was born in New York in 1882. He was an only child.

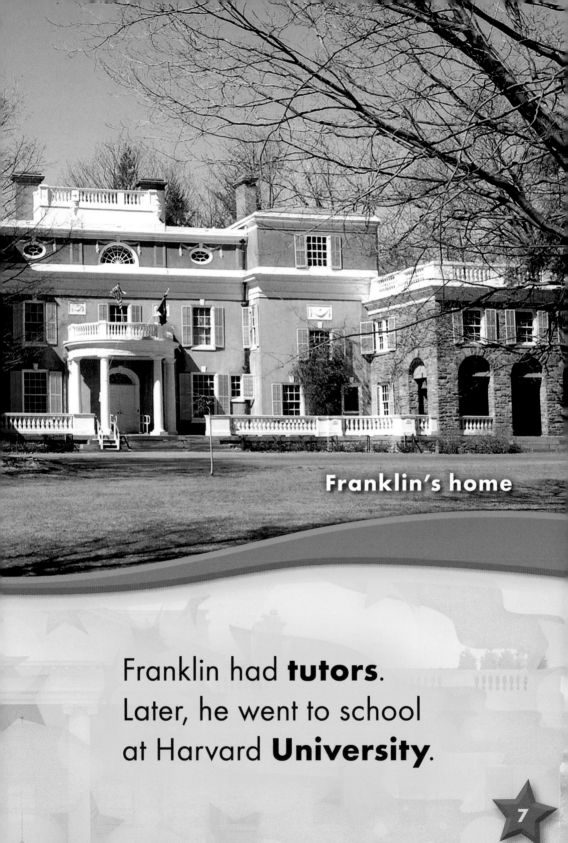

Franklin's home

Franklin had **tutors**.
Later, he went to school
at Harvard **University**.

Franklin studied law
at Columbia University.
He became a **lawyer**.

Presidential Picks

Pets

dogs and horses

Foods

hot dogs and
grilled cheese sandwiches

Sport

swimming

Hobby

stamp collecting

Franklin working as a senator

In 1910, he was **elected** as a New York state **senator**.

Franklin got **polio** in 1921.
He was never able to walk again.

That did not stop him!
He became **governor**
of New York in 1929.

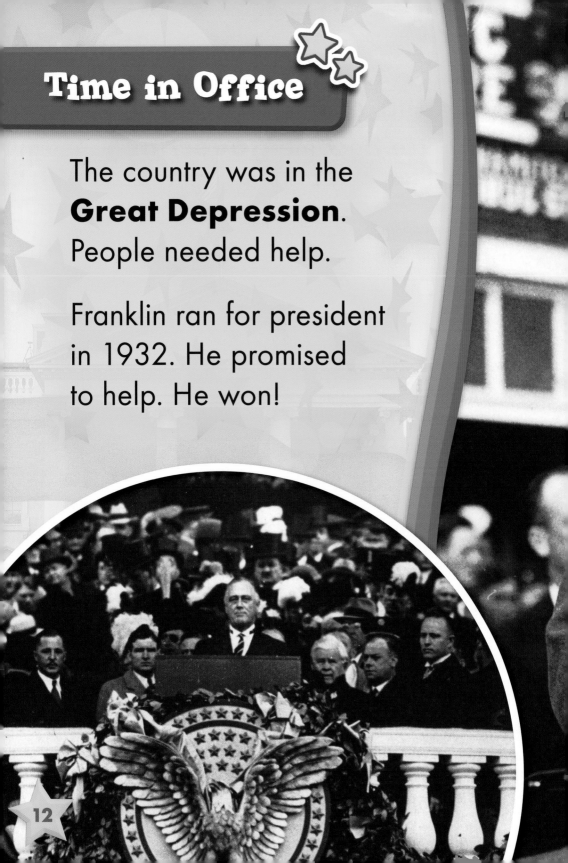

Time in Office

The country was in the **Great Depression**. People needed help.

Franklin ran for president in 1932. He promised to help. He won!

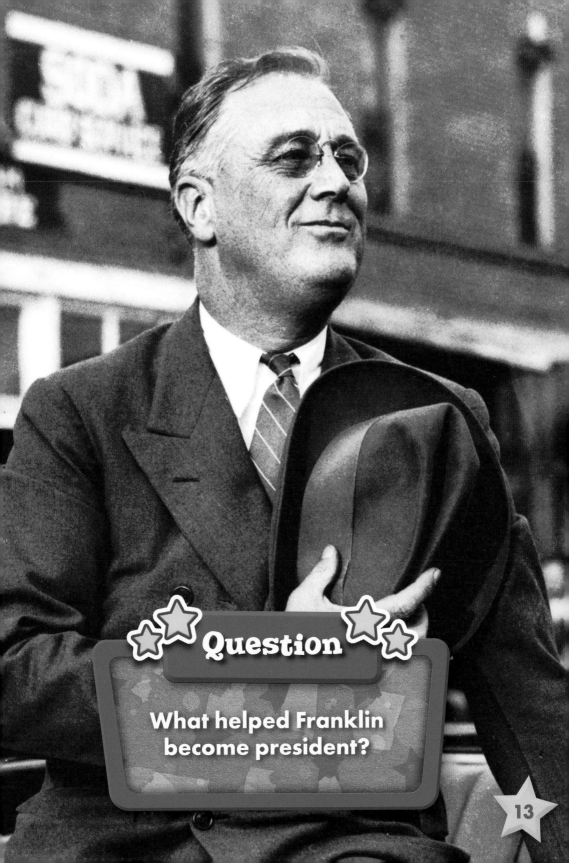

Question

What helped Franklin become president?

13

Franklin kept his promise.
He worked with **Congress**
to make the **New Deal**.

Presidential Profile

Place of Birth

Hyde Park, New York

Schooling

Harvard University and
Columbia University

Birthday

January 30, 1882

Term

1933 to 1945

Party

Democratic

Signature

Vice Presidents

John Garner   Henry Wallace   Harry S. Truman

Franklin tells the nation about the New Deal

It put people back to work.
It helped the **economy**.

In 1939, **World War II** started in Europe. Two years later, Japan attacked the U.S. at Pearl Harbor.

Franklin asked Congress to act. The U.S. entered the war!

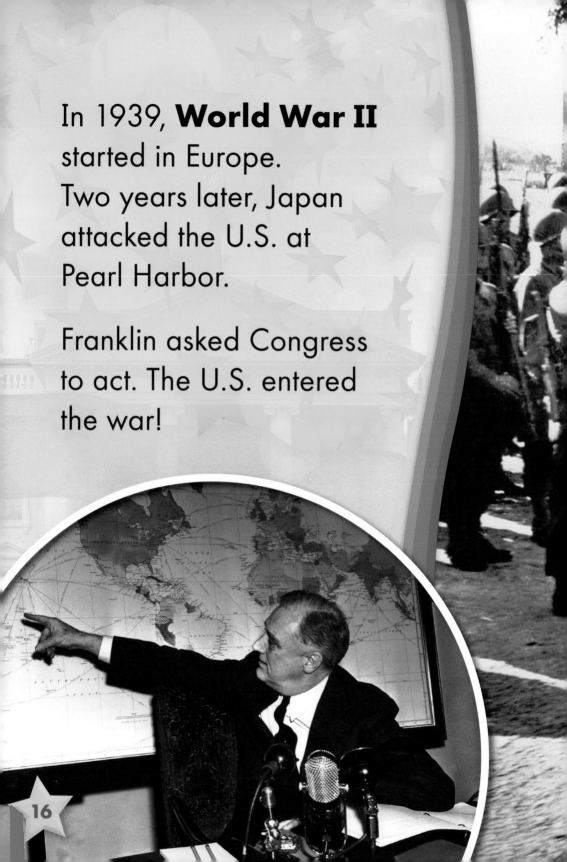

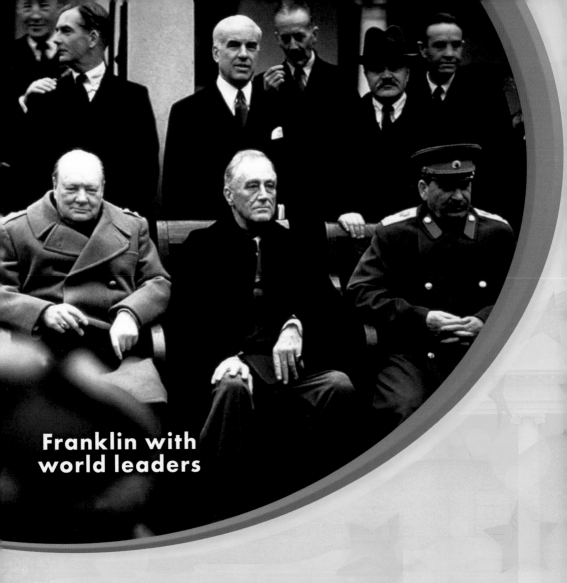

**Franklin with
world leaders**

Franklin worked with
world leaders. They made plans
to win the war. They also started
the **United Nations**. This group
still works to keep world peace.

Franklin Timeline

March 4, 1933

Franklin becomes president and addresses the nation about the New Deal

November 8, 1932

Franklin D. Roosevelt is elected president

December 7, 1941

Japan attacks a U.S. military base in Pearl Harbor, Hawaii

November 7, 1944

Franklin is elected president for the fourth time

April 12, 1945

Franklin dies in office

19

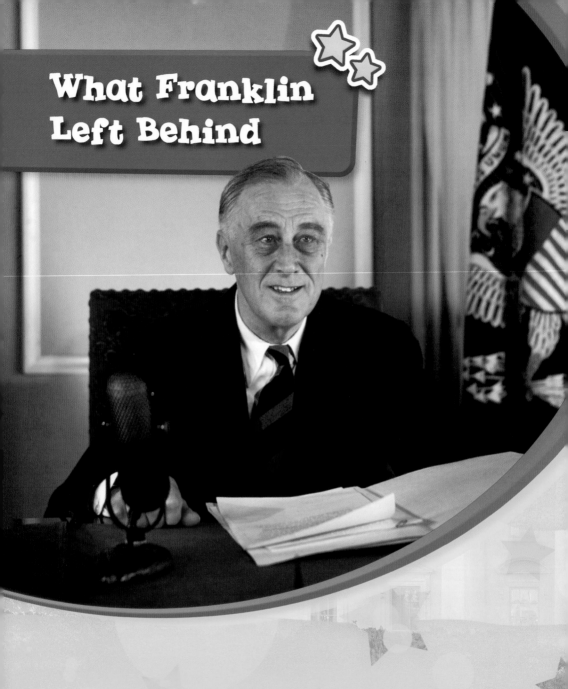

What Franklin Left Behind

Franklin was president for 12 years. He died in 1945.

Franklin was a strong leader. He made the government bigger. He helped a lot of people!

Glossary

Congress—the group of people in the U.S. government who make laws for the country; the United States Senate and House of Representatives are parts of Congress.

economy—the system by which goods and services are made, sold, and bought

elected—chosen by voting

governor—the leader of the government of a state

Great Depression—a period from 1929 to about 1939 when many people lost their jobs, homes, and farms

lawyer—a person trained to help people in a court of law

New Deal—a group of plans that helped the U.S. during the Great Depression

polio—a disease that can make a person unable to move parts of the body

senator—a member of the senate; the senate helps make laws.

tutors—teachers who work with a single student

United Nations—a group of nations that work together for world peace and safety

university—a school that people go to after high school

World War II—the war fought from 1939 to 1945 that involved many countries

To Learn More

AT THE LIBRARY

Dougherty, Steve. *Attack on Pearl Harbor: World War II Strikes Home in the USA*. New York, N.Y.: Scholastic, 2020.

Glenn, Dusk. *Franklin Delano Roosevelt: World War II President*. New York, N.Y.: Children's Press, 2021.

Wilkins, Veronica B. *Great Depression*. Minneapolis, Minn.: Jump!, 2020.

ON THE WEB

FACTSURFER

Factsurfer.com gives you a safe, fun way to find more information.

1. Go to www.factsurfer.com.

2. Enter "Franklin D. Roosevelt " into the search box and click 🔍.

3. Select your book cover to see a list of related content.

Index

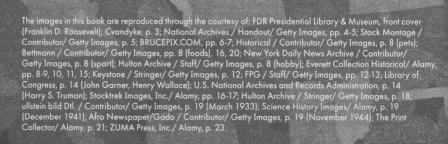

The images in this book are reproduced through the courtesy of: FDR Presidential Library & Museum, front cover (Franklin D. Roosevelt); Cvandyke, p. 3; National Archives / Handout/ Getty Images, pp. 4-5; Stock Montage / Contributor/ Getty Images, p. 5; BRUCEPIX.COM, pp. 6-7; Historical / Contributor/ Getty Images, p. 8 (pets); Bettmann / Contributor/ Getty Images, pp. 8 (foods), 16, 20; New York Daily News Archive / Contributor/ Getty Images, p. 8 (sport); Hulton Archive / Staff/ Getty Images, p. 8 (hobby); Everett Collection Historical/ Alamy, pp. 8-9, 10, 11, 15; Keystone / Stringer/ Getty Images, p. 12; FPG / Staff/ Getty Images, pp. 12-13; Library of Congress, p. 14 (John Garner, Henry Wallace); U.S. National Archives and Records Administration, p. 14 (Harry S. Truman); Stocktrek Images, Inc./ Alamy, pp. 16-17; Hulton Archive / Stringer/ Getty Images, p. 18; ullstein bild Dtl. / Contributor/ Getty Images, p. 19 (March 1933); Science History Images/ Alamy, p. 19 (December 1941); Afro Newspaper/Gado / Contributor/ Getty Images, p. 19 (November 1944); The Print Collector/ Alamy, p. 21; ZUMA Press, Inc./ Alamy, p. 23.